dabble lab

Science
Builders

COMPUTER
PROGRAMMING

LEARN IT, TRY IT!

by Brad Edelman

CAPSTONE PRESS
a capstone imprint

Dabble Lab Books are published by Capstone Press,
1710 Roe Crest Drive, North Mankato, Minnesota 56003
www.mycapstone.com

Library of Congress Cataloging-in-Publication Data
Library of Congress Cataloging-in-Publication data is available on the Library of Congress website.
ISBN 978-1-5157-6424-3 (library binding)
ISBN 978-1-5157-6429-8 (paperback)
ISBN 978-1-5157-6436-6 (eBook PDF)

Editorial Credits
Mandy Robbins, editor; Steve Mead, designer; Kelli Lageson, media researcher; Laura Manthe, production specialist

Photo Credits
Getty Images: The LIFE Picture Collection/Alfred Eisenstaedt, 29; NASA: 11 (top);Shutterstock: 3drenderings, 11 (bottom), AF studio, 41, Africa Studio, 40, Ahmet Misirligul, 10, Antonio Guillem, 33, antoniodiaz, 44, asharkyu, 6, Business stock, 9 (bottom), Dean Drobot, 4, effrosyni, cover, Everett Historical, 8 (top and bottom), Freedom_Studio, 15 (bottom), GaudiLab, 45, Georgejmclittle, 5, goodluz, cover (bottom right), guteksk7, 36, 39, iunewind, cover, 13, 17, Jatinder1990, 12, John Kasawa, 14 (oven), Lane V. Erickson, 20, Leewiew Ponkun, cover (top left), MaluStudio, cover, Mikrobiuz, 30, MSG64, cover, Nick Kinney, cover, Nick Starichenko, cover (top right), Nor Gal, 9 (top), Preto Perola, cover, rangizzz, 43, Ratikova, 14 (bread), 15 (top), Rawpixel.com, 23, Rhonda ODonnell, 28, 31, Sashkin, 35, Stokkete, 19, Tim Jenner, 7, Titima Ongkantong, back cover, 24, 26, VladFree, cover (bottom left), Yurich, 16

Author Dedication
Dedicated to my mother, Edie Edelman. I love you.

Printed in the United States of America.
010373F17

TABLE OF CONTENTS

CHAPTER 1
A World of Technology 4

CHAPTER 2
Computers Throughout
History 7

CHAPTER 3
Amazing Algorithms 13

CHAPTER 4
Bits, Bytes, and Being
Binary 22

CHAPTER 5
Speaking a Computer's
Language 34

CHAPTER 6
Explore Computer
Programming! 44

PROJECT 1
Debug an Algorithm 18

PROJECT 2
Write an Algorithm................. 19

PROJECT 3
Convert Numbers to Binary..... 27

PROJECT 4
Fun With Fonts........................ 32

PROJECT 5
Encryption 42

Glossary..46
Read More...47
Maker Space Tips..47
Internet Sites..47
Index...48
Author Bio...48

CHAPTER 1

A WORLD OF TECHNOLOGY

In today's world, computers are all around us. Things you enjoy every day, such as video games, TV, and the Internet are all possible because of computers.

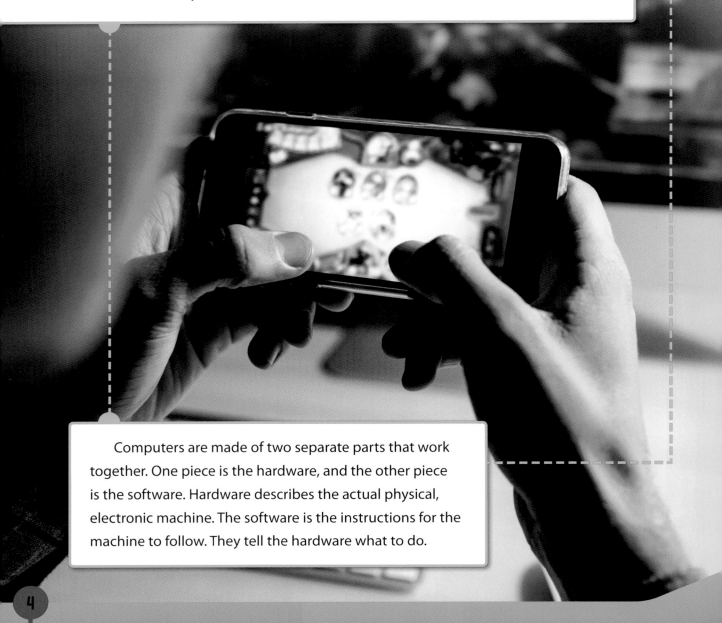

Computers are made of two separate parts that work together. One piece is the hardware, and the other piece is the software. Hardware describes the actual physical, electronic machine. The software is the instructions for the machine to follow. They tell the hardware what to do.

A computer program is another name for software. Think about video games. The video game hardware draws **pixels** on your TV. It detects what buttons you pressed on your controller. The video game software controls everything else. In a basketball video game, it's the computer program that makes the pixels look like a basketball player, and turns a button push into a slam-dunk!

Computers are powerful because they can follow extremely simple step-by-step instructions very quickly. They can also store enormous amounts of information. Computer programmers figure out those steps and how to use that information.

With the help of computer programmers, computer hardware can become something exciting to use and see. Computer programmers have created video games, web **browsers**, social media, online banking websites, and self-driving cars. The possibilities are limited only by your imagination.

pixel—one of the tiny dots on a TV screen or computer monitor that make up the visual image

browser—a software program that lets a user find information, images, and video on the Internet

Computers have become more advanced in the last 50 years. Programs can now turn human speech into text, **synthesize** the human voice, and recognize who is in a photograph. Computers can even use three-dimensional (3-D) printers to create objects from models designed on computers.

You might think computer programming is too difficult for you to understand. But all you need to know is how to read, do math, follow instructions, and think logically. Give it a shot! As a computer programmer, you could help create the technology of the future.

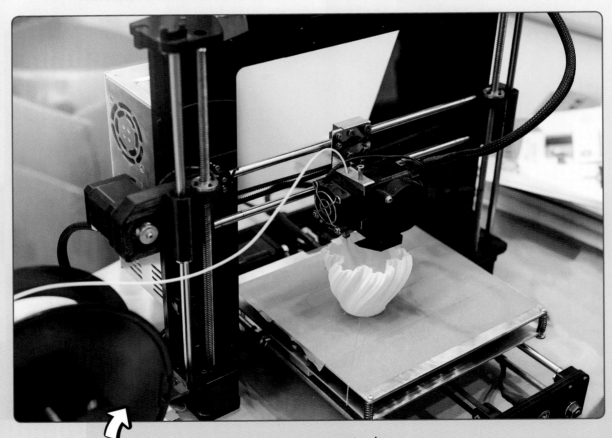

3-D printers print out objects one layer at a time.

synthesize—to create something in an unnatural way, such as converting typed text into spoken words

CHAPTER 2

COMPUTERS THROUGHOUT HISTORY

It may seem hard to believe, but less than 100 years ago, computers as we know them today did not exist. Yet for hundreds of years, humans have built clever machines to help with tasks. The abacus was invented more than 2,000 years ago to help with mathematics. The sextant was a tool sailors used to navigate the ocean. People even built machines that used gears and levers to do math equations. But none of these inventions were nearly as advanced as modern-day computers.

In the mid-1800s, Charles Babbage and Ava Lovelace produced some of the earliest work that resembles today's computers and computer programs. They designed a general purpose programmable machine. Because it was so complex for its time, they couldn't figure out how to build their machine. But the ideas they had were so good that programmers still use them today.

1890

In the late 1800s, Herman Hollerith found a way to use punch cards to help collect the data needed for the 1890 U.S. Census. The punch cards had originally been used to control machines that wove patterned fabric. Those punch cards became a part of early computer programming and remained part of it through the 1960s and 1970s.

In 1946 scientists at the University of Pennsylvania finished building the Electronic Numerical Integrator And Computer (ENIAC). It is considered by many to be the first modern electronic computer. The ENIAC filled a large room and weighed 30 tons (27 metric tons). It could make 5,000 calculations per second, which is far fewer than today's computers. It cost nearly $500,000 at the time.

1946

1980s

By the mid-1980s, desktop computers such as the IBM PC and Apple Macintosh had become common tools in businesses and schools. These computers could perform millions of calculations per second. But they used bulky video displays and hard-to-learn keyboard commands. And while they were less expensive than the ENIAC had cost to build, they still cost thousands of dollars.

Today more than 2 billion people world-wide have smart phones or tablets. These modern computers are small and lightweight. They perform billions of calculations per second and have easy-to-use touch screens with video and 3-D graphics. They cost hundreds of dollars.

TODAY

Industry experts expect this trend to continue. Computers will get more powerful and less expensive. They have even begun to find their way into everyday objects such as light bulbs and eye glasses.

FACT

A NASA computer programmer named Margaret Hamilton wrote the flight software for the Apollo Space Program. Her code made it possible to land people on the moon in the 1960s.

COMPANY CONTRIBUTIONS

In addition to individual people, there have been many companies that have made important contributions to the development of modern computing. Bell Labs developed the telephone, satellite communications, and the cell phone. They also created the transistor. A transistor is a tiny switch that is only activated when a third wire has electricity in it. It allows electrical engineers to control the flow of electricity in a device. Without the invention of the transistor, today's computers would not be possible.

Intel, IBM, and Microsoft worked together to make the IBM PC. It was the first home or work computer for millions of people in the 1980s.

Apple created the first mainstream desktop computer, the Apple][. They also developed the Macintosh desktop computer, the iPod, iPhone, and iPad.

It may be hard to imagine, but computers didn't always have touch screens like today's tablets and smart phones. They didn't even display graphics or pictures. Computers used to require complicated commands typed letter-by-letter on a keyboard. Then Xerox PARC created graphical user interfaces, made popular by Apple and Microsoft. This innovation let users click on images on the screen. The idea of just pointing at a picture with a mouse or your finger made computers much friendlier and easier to use.

Google created the search engine of the same name, which makes it easy to find nearly anything on the Internet. In 2005 Google Maps was released, giving people directions to any location in the world. Google bought YouTube in 2006, which lets users share videos with people all over the world.

CHAPTER 3

AMAZING ALGORITHMS

As computers became more capable, people had to get more clever about how to tell them what to do. An algorithm is a series of steps that tells a computer how to do a task. The electronic **circuits** inside the computer only know how to do very simple things. For example, the hardware can do things such as add two numbers or see if two numbers are equal, and if they are, do one thing, and if they aren't, do another thing. That is called branching.

The computer follows instructions exactly. It does not consider whether something seems wrong or out of order. It does not realize if a step is missing. A computer is just a machine. It does not think like a person.

circuit—the complete path of an electrical current

CREATE YOUR OWN ALGORITHM

Try to make a real-life algorithm. For example, let's say your friend asked for a list of the steps needed to make a piece of toast.

You might start with:

ALGORITHM 1

1. Put bread in the toaster oven.
2. Press toast button.

⇧

These instructions might be clear enough for a person, but they wouldn't be for a computer. If your friend acted like a computer, she might put the entire loaf of bread, including its plastic bag into the toaster oven. After all, you didn't say to take a slice of bread out of the bag!

ALGORITHM 2

So then you add to the list:

1. Take a slice of bread out of the bag.
2. Put the slice of bread into the toaster oven.
3. Press toast button.

Your friend, still acting like a computer, gets stuck on step 1. She asks, "How do I get a slice of bread out of the bag? The bag has no opening."

ALGORITHM 3

So you add to the list again:

1. Open the bread bag by untwisting and removing the tie.
2. Take a slice of bread out of the bag.
3. Put the slice of bread into the toaster oven.
4. Press toast button.

The next day you find the rest of your bag of bread has gone stale because you did not specifically tell your friend to close the bag again.

FUNCTIONS AND LOOPS

You're probably starting to get the idea. For a computer program to work, every detail must be explained thoroughly. Computer programmers learn techniques to do this efficiently. For example, if you wanted to make 10 pieces of toast, you would not write out all the steps 10 times. That would be a lot more work, and rewriting the commands every time would leave room for mistakes. It would also be difficult to make changes. If you wanted to add butter, you'd have to go back and add that step 10 times.

Instead you could create a function called "MakeToast." A function is an algorithm that has already been written and named. Programmers can insert them into their programs to save time. Programmers also use loops. A loop will run a function repeatedly. You could program your "MakeToast" function to run 10 times in a loop.

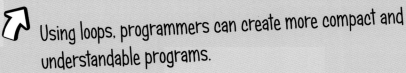 Using loops, programmers can create more compact and understandable programs.

FINDING THE BUGS

Mistakes in computer programs are called bugs. Rumor has it that one of the first computers ever built stopped working because of a bug crawling into the circuits. Programmers now joke that there must be a bug in the computer if a program isn't working correctly.

Even the best computer programmers make mistakes and have to **debug** their program. The mistakes can be with the **logic** itself. For example, you can forget to take something into account, such as taking the bread out of the bag to make toast. Or sometimes, the mistake can just be a typo.

debug—to search for a mistake in an algorithm
logic—careful and correct reasoning and thinking

DEBUG AN ALGORITHM

Do you think you could find a bug in a program? This algorithm shows the steps that a kid might use to get dressed for school in the morning. But it doesn't quite work. See if you can debug it!

GET DRESSED FOR SCHOOL

Take a shower.

Dry off with a towel.

Put on underwear.

Put on pants.

Put on shirt.

Put on shoes.

Put on socks.

Tie shoes.

It might not have been obvious at first, but you probably figured out how to debug the algorithm. You can't put socks on over shoes, after all.

Challenge

How does this list of steps compare to your own process for getting ready in the morning? Are there any steps missing? Is there any way to be more specific in the list of steps? Go through and improve this algorithm.

WRITE AN ALGORITHM

Now that you've debugged an algorithm, see if you can make your own. Write an algorithm for how to brush your teeth. What steps are involved? Be as detailed as possible about all the steps. Then go to the bathroom and follow your algorithm. Or better yet, have someone else follow it.

Challenge

Review your algorithm. Are there any steps you may have missed? Even tiny bugs can make a big difference. Go back and debug your program if necessary.

COMPUTER ALGORITHMS

You've seen some real-life examples of algorithms. Now let's take a look at a computer algorithm. Algorithms can be the difference between computer functions taking minutes, hours, or even years.

Imagine you have a list of 1,000 names, and you need to put them into alphabetical order. What is the best way to do it? How many steps would it take?

Alphabetizing names on a computer uses a sorting algorithm. Computer programmers have studied different ways of doing this. Some ways are much more efficient than others.

How would you explain the process of sorting a list in steps? You could look through the entire list, and find the name that comes first. Then you could do that again and again until there are no more names left. How many steps would that take? The first time, there are 1,000 names to go through. The next time there are 999. To find the total number of steps you would add 1,000+999+998, and so on, until you get to number 1. In total, that would be more than 500,000 steps!

A different method is to split the list in half. Then half it again, and again until each grouping was only two items. It's very easy to sort two items alphabetically. Also when you have two pre-sorted lists you can **merge** them because it requires only deciding from which list to take the next name. This method would require only about 10,000 steps — far fewer than the previous algorithm.

So for a list of 1,000 names, it's 50 times less work. With a list of a million names, it would be 50,000 times less work. Wow!

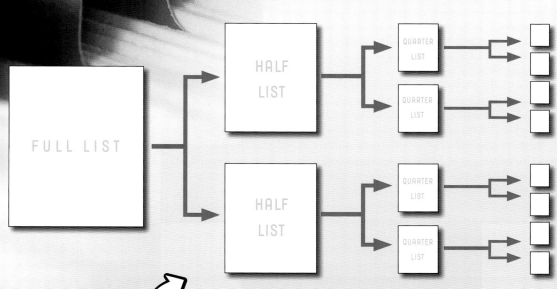

FULL LIST

HALF LIST

HALF LIST

QUARTER LIST

QUARTER LIST

QUARTER LIST

QUARTER LIST

Splitting lists in half quickly breaks a large project into smaller, more manageable parts.

CHAPTER 4

BITS, BYTES, AND BEING BINARY

Think about a light bulb. When you turn it on you use a switch. The switch lets electricity flow through a wire. When the electricity is flowing, the light bulb turns on. When it is not, the light bulb turns off. The light bulb has two states — on and off. In this same way, the tiny wires inside a computer can be on and off. When something can only exist in one of two states, it is referred to as binary.

Computer programmers call a binary value a **bit**. And instead of calling the two states on and off, programmers use numbers. Off is represented as "0," and on is represented as "1." With 1 bit, we can represent one of two numbers, either 0 or 1.

What if we wanted more than two options? Use more bits!

If we use two bits there are four combinations possible:	With three bits there are 8 combinations possible:
00	000
01	001
10	010
11	011
	100
	101
	110
	111

bit—a single binary value; in computer programming that value is either zero or one

byte—a collection of 8-bits that can represent 256 different states; 1,024 bytes Is called a kilobyte

All of the information inside of a computer is coded into bits, from text to music and images. The more complex the information, the more bits are needed to represent it.

It would be overwhelming to refer to computed information as nothing but a series of bits. So computer programmers group bits together into bigger pieces, such as a **byte**, a **megabyte** (MB), or a **gigabyte** (GB).

These terms are used to describe how much information can be stored or used by a computer. Today's computers store gigabytes and even **terabytes** of information.

megabyte—a collection of 1,024 kilobytes   **terabyte**—a collection of 1,024 gigabytes

gigabyte—a collection of 1,024 megabytes

DATA TYPES

Bytes can be even more useful when divided into data types. Data types are collections of bytes that represent a bigger piece of information. For example, a character is a string of bytes that represent either a letter, the numbers zero through nine, or a symbol. The letter A is represented as 01000001. A string refers to a series of characters, such as a word or a sentence.

For example, this is what the words "ice cream" look like in bits and bytes:

```
01001001  =  I
01000011  =  C
01000101  =  E
00100000  =
01000011  =  C
01010010  =  R
01000101  =  E
01000001  =  A
01001101  =  M
```

It's a lot easier for a programmer to refer to the string "ICE CREAM" than it is to list the bits and bytes that represent it. That's why data types are so useful.

Whole numbers, that is numbers that do not have decimals or fractions, are typically represented by the integer data type. An integer is a sequence of bytes that represents a whole number. It takes four bytes to represent numbers from roughly negative 2 billion to positive 2 billion.

When it comes to numbers that are more than one digit, it's helpful to imagine them being held in columns. The typical columns of a number represent ones, tens, hundreds, thousands, and so on. Each column is worth 10 times the previous column. So the number 325 could be represented as:

100s	10s	1s
3	2	5

In other words, in the number 325, there are three 100s, two 10s, and five 1s.

BINARY NUMBERS

...s are also helpful when converting the decimal numbers you use ...to binary numbers. Because numbers in a computer can only be ... by 0 or 1, their columns are set up differently. Instead of a system ...column is multiplied by 10, they use a system where each column ...alue. Each column is worth two times the previous column. And ...) possible values per column (0 to 9), there are only two possible ...olumn (0 or 1).

...is what the column values would be in binary:

512	256	128	64	32	16	8	4	2	1

To convert a number to binary you would ask yourself how many times the number in a column goes into the number you're trying to convert. The answer could only be 0 or 1. Take the number 5, for example. You would start your binary code in the 4 column. Why? Any larger number doesn't go into five. Any smaller number would go into it more than once. Four goes into five one time, so you would write a 1 in that column. When you subtract 4 from five, you have 1 left. So you would put 1 in the 1 column, and zero in the 2 column. So for the number 5 in binary, you would use the bits 101:

4	2	1
1	0	1

$$(1\times4) + (0\times2) + (1\times1) = 5$$

CONVERT NUMBERS TO BINARY

Create a chart to help you visualize the number columns for representing an integer in binary code. Each column represents a bit. It should look like this:

8	4	2	1	= number
			1	1
		1	0	2
		1	1	3
	1	0	0	4

Fill in the blank boxes with the binary numbers for the numbers 5 to 15. The first four rows are filled in for you. See if you can complete the chart.

Challenge

Write the binary number for the year you were born. This will take 11 columns, or bits, and you may need a calculator. It helps to start from the left side and work your way down to 1.

CONVERTING IMAGES TO BITS

Converting bits to numbers is one thing. But how do computer programmers represent images in 0's and 1's? They use pixels.

A digital photo is nothing but a grid of pixels. The smaller you make the pixels, the clearer the **digital** representation will be.

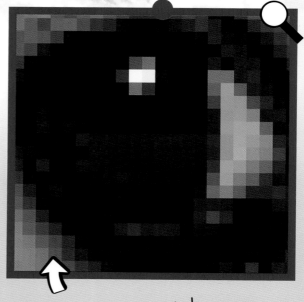

When you zoom in on pixels you can see how each square is a single color.

28

A digital original and a digital copy are truly the same. When copying anything that isn't digital, the copy is always slightly different, but digital copies are always perfect.

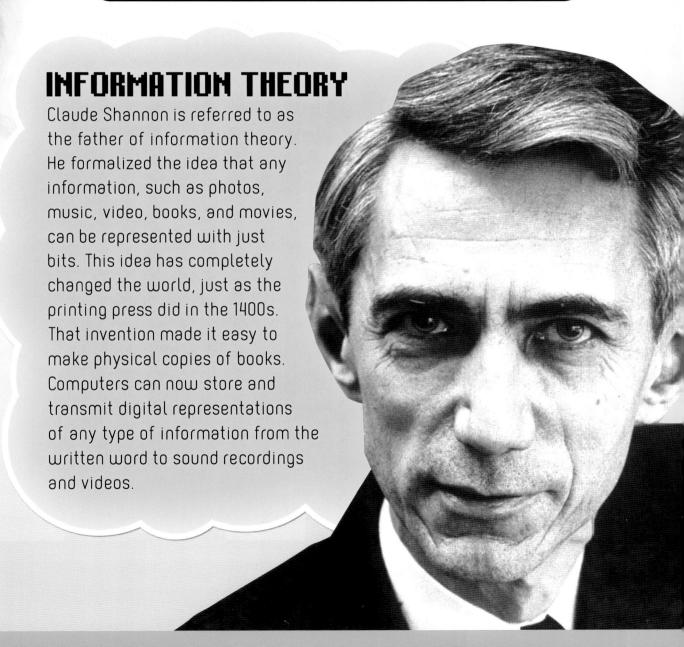

INFORMATION THEORY

Claude Shannon is referred to as the father of information theory. He formalized the idea that any information, such as photos, music, video, books, and movies, can be represented with just bits. This idea has completely changed the world, just as the printing press did in the 1400s. That invention made it easy to make physical copies of books. Computers can now store and transmit digital representations of any type of information from the written word to sound recordings and videos.

digital—a type of information that is made of bits and can be copied exactly

PICKING APART PIXELS

Each square pixel of an image's grid is one color. The smaller the pixels are, the easier it is to pick a single color. If the pixel is too big, the programmer picks a color that is the best match for that area, but the overall image can end up looking blurry.

Computers think about colors as red, green, or blue (RGB) values. That refers to how much red, green, and blue light would be mixed to recreate a particular color. Think about mixing colored light as similar to mixing colored paint, but the colors combine a little bit differently.

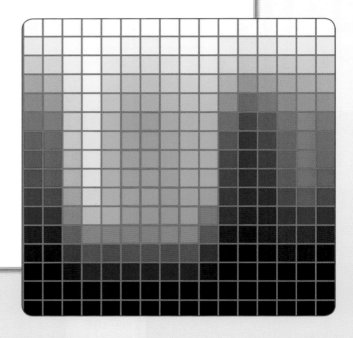

In programming, colors have from 0 to 255 intensity of each color of light. Programmers think of zero as its own number. Because zero is included, it's 256 different values. It takes 8 bits of data to communicate that many values. There are three different colors that can be represented with 8 bits. If you multiply 3 x 8 you get 24. So colors can be represented with 24 bits of data.

Now let's convert those colors into an image. Imagine a photo being placed into a grid of 16 by 16 pixels. If you multiply 16 x 16 you get 256. Each pixel is represented by 24 bits. So you multiply 256 x 24, which equals 6,144. That means your image will be made up of 6,144 bits of information.

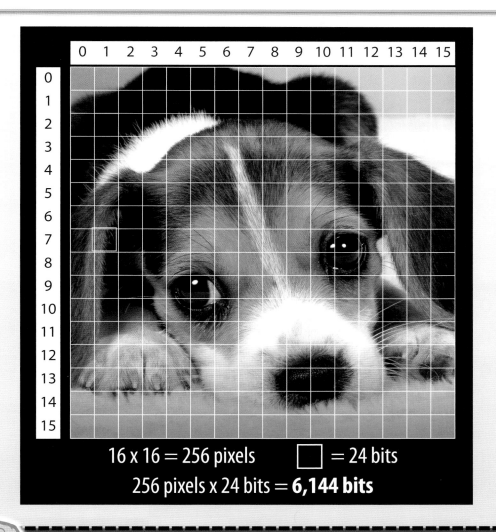

16 x 16 = 256 pixels   ☐ = 24 bits
256 pixels x 24 bits = **6,144 bits**

Challenge

If a smartphone takes 10 megapixel photos, that means it turns a photo into 10 million pixels of 24 bits each. Can you figure out how many bits that would be? How many bytes would it be?

(Answer: 240 million bits/30 million bytes)

FUN WITH FONTS

Take what you've learned about converting pixels to images to create a simple **font**. A font may represent letters, but each letter is also its own image. Once a font is created, computers can use pixels to draw letters and words on the screen.

Imagine that each letter of the alphabet can be represented using a 5x5 grid of pixels. Black is represented by 1, and white is represented by 0. So the letter "T" might look like this grid:

1	1	1	1	1
0	0	1	0	0
0	0	1	0	0
0	0	1	0	0
0	0	1	0	0

So for the letter "T" in this font, the computer could use these 25 bits to know how to draw the letter on the screen. Here's each row, left-to-right, top-to-bottom. Remember, black is 1, white is 0:

1111100100001000010000100

Or perhaps the word "CAT" would look like:

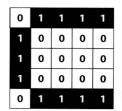
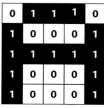

Can you write the binary data for the three letters needed in the font for "CAT?"

FACT

The font you used is a fairly simple font. To make a nicer looking font you would need more pixels.

Challenge

Now make 5x5 grids in which you can write your own name.
You could even use graph paper to make it easier.

TAKE A BYTE OUT OF MUSIC

Do you think it's possible that there are only so many ways musicians can create a song? Technically, it's true, but there are so many that we're not in danger of running of out of great new music.

You probably know what compact disks (CDs) are. They store sound recordings. The binary format used on CDs takes 176,400 bytes for each second of music. Keep in mind that 1 byte equals 8 bits. There are 60 seconds in a minute, and the average song is around 4 minutes long. The equation to figure out how many bytes there are in a 4-minute song is:

$$176,400 \text{ (bytes)} \times 60 \text{ (seconds)} \times 4 \text{ (minutes)} = 42,336,000 \text{ bytes}$$

You can convert 42,336,000 bytes to about 42 megabytes (MB). That's an enormous about of bits, but it's still a limited number. So technically, there is a limited number of songs possible. But that number is still large enough to include any 4-minute song ever recorded.

font—a stylized typeface used to draw text on a screen or print it to paper

CHAPTER 5

SPEAKING A COMPUTER'S LANGUAGE

In the earlier projects, you wrote algorithms in English. However, when computer programmers write an algorithm, they write them in a computer language. Computer languages have far fewer words and are much more precise than spoken languages. To understand why, consider the sentence:

I saw a man on a hill with a telescope.

What does it mean?

1. There's a man on a hill, and I'm watching him with my telescope.

or

2. I see a man on a hill who has a telescope.

If you read this text in a book, you could probably figure out which option was true by paying attention to clues in the sentences around it. But computers don't have that intuitive ability. This is why computer languages are very precise.

Some examples of computer languages are JavaScript, Python, and Ruby. Computer languages have fewer words than spoken languages. They rely more on symbols and numbers. The words they do use are keywords. They clarify how the computer uses the symbols and numbers. For example, some of the keywords in the JavaScript computer language are "if," "for," "while," and "function."

MULTIPLE COMPUTER LANGUAGES

Just like there are many spoken languages, there are also many computer languages. It's a good idea to learn multiple computer languages. You can learn to write your logic in multiple ways. Some languages may be better for expressing some ideas than others. Think about it like music. A musician can play a melody on the guitar or on the trombone. It will probably sound better or play more easily on one than the other, depending on the tune. Just like musicians can play multiple instruments, a computer programmer can express an idea in multiple computer languages.

READING COMPUTER LANGUAGES

Spoken languages use periods, commas, quotation marks, question marks, and other symbols to more clearly communicate ideas. Computer programming languages do this also. The way they use symbols and form sentences is called syntax and grammar.

Let's try to understand some code written in JavaScript. In JavaScript, curly braces such as these { } are used to group statements together. It's sort of like showing where a paragraph begins and ends. A function is a command that asks a program to perform a certain task. One example in JavaScript is the command "console.log". This function asks the program to print something for you to read on the screen.

Computers can do amazingly complex things, but at their core they only perform extremely simple operations. They include:

```
▶ basic math — addition, subtraction,
  multiplication, and division

▶ comparing for equality or inequality

▶ performing an action only if something else
  is true

▶ performing an action repeatedly

▶ naming a sequence of steps so it can be reused
  easily. This is called a function.

▶ creating a named "variable" to hold a value.
  For example, we could say x=4, and then use x
  instead of 4. If x is used in many places, we
  could change to x=5, by changing code in only
  one place rather than in many.
```

This is how these simple operations look in JavaScript:

A Variable and Basic Math

```
var x = 4 + 2;
```
So x now means **6**.

```
var y = x * 3;
```
So y now means **18**.

`var` means I'm about to give a name for a variable.

The = sign means "assign" what comes next to the variable.

The + means add. The * means multiply. The ; means the sentence is over — like a period in English.

COMPARING FOR EQUALITY AND INEQUALITY

Because the single equals sign is used for assigning a name or value to a variable, programmers use the double equals sign to ask if two things are equal. For example:

3 == 1+2

is true, because 1+2 is 3. But:

4 == 1+2

is false. However,

4 > 1+2

is true because 4 is greater than 3.

USING PARENTHESES

Parentheses are used to indicate values that should be grouped together. For example, you might use parentheses to tell the computer what an **"if"** statement should consider, or what a function should use. For example:

```
if (2 + 2 == 4) {
  console.log("hello");
}
```

WILL print "hello," but

```
if (2 + 2 == 5) {
  console.log("hello");
}
```

will NOT print hello. Do you see why? **2+2==4** is true, but **2+2==5** is false.

BUILDING LOGIC

It's the art of software engineering to learn how to build small pieces of logic into bigger functions. Those functions can be put together to build larger and larger functions. How these decisions are made is one of the most important aspects of computer programming and all types of engineering.

We can build up logic from the basic concepts you've learned about computer programming.

For example, imagine you want a computer to add up all the numbers from 1 to **n**. The letter "**n**" stands for any positive number you choose. Imagine you chose the number 10. That means you want to know the answer to the equation:

$$1+2+3+4+5+6+7+8+9+10$$

This is how you would write that command in JavaScript, with a line-by-line explanation:

Open curly brace to start the list of instructions inside the function.

Create a variable named "`result`" to hold the sum. Start it at 0.

The keyword "`while`" is a type of loop — a way of doing steps repeatedly while something is true. If n is `10` and we're counting with `i`, it's like saying, is `1<10`, ok, is `2<10`, ok… `10<=10` ok, but `11<=10` is not, so it stops.

Close curly brace stops the list of instructions inside the loop.

Close curly brace stops the list of instructions inside the function.

38

Give the function a name and show it takes one input, which we'll call "n", the highest number we want to add.

Create a variable named "i" to use for counting.

Open curly brace to start the list of instructions to repeat inside the loop.

```
function printSum(n)
{
    var result = 0;
    var i = 1;
    while (i <= n) {
        result = result + i;
        i = i + 1;
    }
console.log(result);
}
```

Add i to the "result" sum.

Move "i" to the next number... so if i was 1, it becomes 2. If it was 9, it becomes 10.

Print the result so the human can see it.

RUNNING A PROGRAM

You have some of the building blocks of computer programming now. So you might wonder how a computer actually runs a program. Generally speaking, computers can do only a limited number of small operations defined by their **microprocessor**. This is the primary computer chip inside of it.

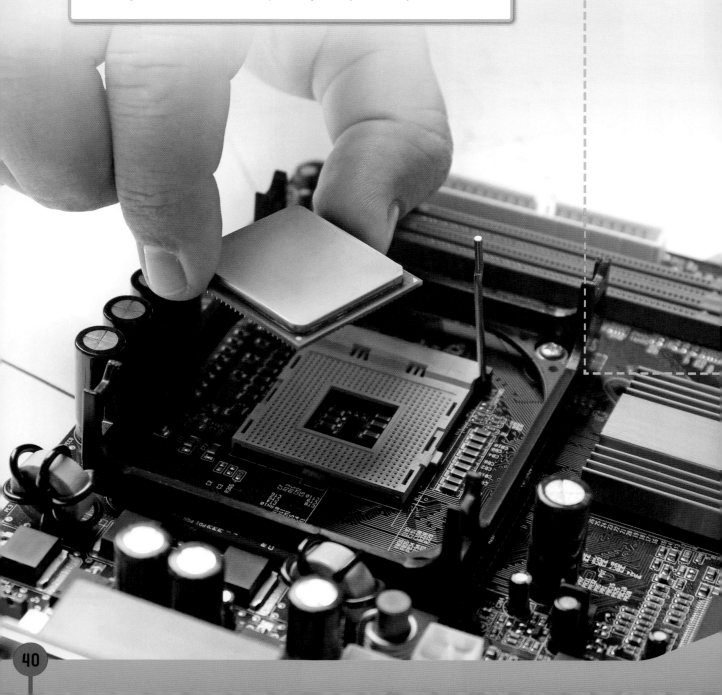

STANDING ON THE SHOULDERS OF GIANTS

Scientists commonly use the phrase "stand on the shoulders of giants." What does that mean? It means that by using the work of the people who came before you, you can build on what they've done to reach even greater heights. Computer programmers don't have to write every program from scratch. They use collections of functions already written by others. These collections are often referred to as a library or a framework.

JPG

Consider something such as a photo on your smart phone. It is often stored as a "JPEG Image." JPEG stands for "Joint Photographic Experts Group." JPEG allows a picture to be saved in a way that takes significantly less storage. Creating this image format took five to 10 years of development by dozens of brilliant engineers. Now, it's a well-defined format that's easy to use for everyone.

Originally, programmers had to write out their logic in the 0's and 1's directly understood by the computer hardware. That means typing out thousands upon thousands of bits of information by hand. To make programming easier, programmers have created tools such as compilers and interpreters. These special computer programs turn other programs written in languages such as Python and JavaScript into the 0's and 1's needed by the computer. Early compilers made it easier to design better languages, which in turn made it easier to make better compilers. This repetitive process of improvement is called "bootstrapping."

microprocessor—a tiny computer processor contained in an electronic computer chip

ENCRYPTION

Throughout history, people have sent secret messages. Computers make this both easier and harder. For example, one way to **encode** a secret message is a substitution **cipher**. In this approach, each letter of the alphabet is replaced with a different letter. Perhaps all `Es` would become `Rs`. A computer can make encoding and decoding the message much faster. But it also makes it easier for someone without knowledge of the code to discover the secret message.

Use this substitution cipher to decode the message below. For each letter in the encoded message, find which letter to replace it with based on this table. For example, the first letter "**S**" was the replacement for the letter "**C**".

A	B	C	D	E	F	G	H	I	J	K	L	M
M	U	S	E	W	P	J	A	Z	R	N	F	G

N	O	P	Q	R	S	T	U	V	W	X	Y	Z
B	I	V	L	X	Q	K	O	Y	T	H	D	C

SIBJXMKOFMKZIBQ! DIO MXW KAZBNZBJ FZNW M SIGVOKWX VXIJXMGGWX.

Encryption is very important in today's world. When people use the Internet, they may transmit secret information such as passwords or credit card numbers. For this information to be sent secretly, encryption is used.

Mathematicians and computer programmers have worked together to come up with sophisticated algorithms that are much harder to figure out than a substitution cipher. These algorithms are based on complex mathematics.

Highly advanced methods of encryption are used to keep credit card information private on the Internet.

encode—to convert a written message into code

cipher—a secret or disguised way of writing

CHAPTER 6

EXPLORE COMPUTER PROGRAMMING!

Computer programming is a fun and exciting field of study with many possibilities. It can be a useful skill and a great way to improve your logical thinking. You could even make it your career some day.

TEAMWORK

Many people think computer programmers spend hours alone in front of a computer. Sometimes that's true, but there is also a lot of teamwork involved. Programmers work with graphic designers, marketers, other experts, and even customers to make the best technology possible.

Computer programmers also need to work with people in different parts of a company. People in business, marketing, sales and product management identify projects, help specify the details, and guide products to market. It takes a whole team of people to create, market, and sell great software.

PRACTICAL PROGRAMS

The types of software that programmers create can vary greatly. For example, some programs used in schools are written and used for a day, a week, or a semester. Other types of programs used in business are used for many years. It's important that a program be easily understood both by its original author and by others. That way it can be easily changed, updated, and corrected in the future.

Computer programming is a challenging, rewarding, fun activity you can enjoy for a lifetime. You have some of the basics now, so keep learning, and see where computer programming can take you!

GLOSSARY

bit (BIT)—a single binary value; in computer programming that value is either zero or one

browser (BROWZ-uhr)—a software program that lets a user find information, images, and video on the Internet

byte (BYTE)—a collection of 8-bits that can represent 256 different states; 1,024 bytes is called a kilobyte

cipher (SY-fur)—a secret or disguised way of writing

circuit (SUHR-kuht)—the complete path of an electrical current

debug (dee-BUHG)—to search for a mistake in an algorithm

digital (DI-juh-tuhl)—information made of bits that can be copied exactly

encode (en-KOHD)—to convert a written message into code

font (FONT)—a set of letters and symbols in a particular design

gigabyte (GIH-guh-byte)—a collection of 1,024 megabytes

logic (LOJ-ik)—careful and correct reasoning and thinking

megabyte (MEG-uh-byte)—a collection of 1,024 kilobytes

merge (MURJ)—to unite two or more things

microprocessor (my-kro-PROSS-ess-uhr)—a tiny computer processor contained in an electronic computer chip

pixel (PIKS-uhl)—one of the tiny dots on a video screen or computer monitor that make up the visual image

synthesize (SIN-thuh-size)—to create something in an unnatural way, such as converting typed text into spoken words

terabyte (TAYR-uh-byte)—a collection of 1,024 gigabytes

READ MORE

Briggs, Jason R. *Python for Kids: A Playful Introduction to Programming.* San Francisco: No Starch Press, 2013.

Wallmark, Laurie. *Ada Byron Lovelace and the Thinking Machine.* Berkeley: Creston Books, 2015.

Woodcock, Jon. *Coding Games in Scratch: A Step-By-Step Visual Guide to Building Your Own Computer Games.* New York: DK Children, 2015

MAKER SPACE TIPS

Download tips and tricks for using this book and others in a library maker space.

Visit *www.capstonepub.com/dabblelabresources*

INTERNET SITES

Use FactHound to find Internet sites related to this book.

Visit *www.facthound.com*

Just type in 9781515764243 and go.

Check out projects, games and lots more at
www.capstonekids.com

INDEX

algorithms, 13–14, 16, 18–21, 34, 43

Apple, 9, 11, 12

Babbage, Charles, 7

Bell Labs, 11

bugs, 17, 18, 19

computer languages, 34–37, 41
  JavaScript, 34, 36, 37, 38, 41

data types, 24, 25

Electronic Numerical Integrator
  And Computer (ENIAC), 8, 9

encryption, 42–43

functions, 16, 20, 34, 36–39, 41

Google, 12

Hamilton, Margaret, 11

hardware, 4, 5, 13, 41

Hollerith, Herman, 8

IBM, 9, 11

Intel, 11

loops, 16, 38, 39

Lovelace, Ava, 7

microprocessors, 40

Microsoft, 11, 12

pixels, 5, 28, 30, 31, 32

Shannon, Claude, 29

software, 4, 5, 11, 38, 45

Xerox PARC, 12

AUTHOR BIO

Brad Edelman is a software developer and entrepreneur. He earned a Bachelor's degree in Computer Science and Engineering from the Massachusetts Institute of Technology and holds 12 patents. Brad squandered much of his childhood programming his Apple][+ and endured many years of "geek ridicule" before the Internet made computers cool.

Brad has spent the past 25 years working in Silicon Valley. He has helped develop many products including Adobe PageMill, shockwave.com, Macromedia Flash (especially video capabilities), and Adobe Connect. He also helped build the startup companies PlayFirst (Diner Dash) and Fingerprint Digital (Samsung Kids).

Currently, Brad works at Salesforce.com where he helps manage and develop their database infrastructure. He lives in Lafayette, California, with his wife and children. In addition to his career and family, Brad enjoys playing basketball and guitar.